the PATH *to* PROSPERITY

the PATH *to* PROSPERITY

James Allen

The Path to Prosperity by James Allen
Public Domain. Reprint edition by Sound Wisdom, 2022

Published and Distributed by
SOUND WISDOM
PO Box 310, Shippensburg, PA 17257-0310
717-530-2122
info@soundwisdom.com
www.soundwisdom.com

Printed in the USA

Annotated by John Martin and Jennifer Janechek, PhD

ISBN 13: 978-1-64095-140-2
ISBN eBook: 978-1-64095-141-9

Note: This book is a product of its time and does not reflect the same views on race, gender, sexuality, ethnicity, and interpersonal relations as it would if it were written today.

For Worldwide Distribution, Printed in the U.S.A.
1 2 3 4 5 6 / 25 24 23 22

TABLE OF CONTENTS

CHAPTER 1

THE LESSON OF EVIL

"Your pain is the breaking of the shell that encloses your understanding."

—KAHLIL GIBRAN

REALITY CHECK

Stress, pain, and sadness are the shadows of life. Everyone in the world has felt the sting of pain. Each person has experienced a troubled, worried mind. Everyone has felt the hot tears of unspeakable sadness. The "Great Destroyers," disease and death, have barged into every home ripping heart from heart and throwing the dark blanket of gloom over everyone inside.

Everyone is caught in the inescapable meshes of evil. Misery and misfortune lie in wait for every individual.

Most people try to escape the bad things in life by doing things that only trap them further or lead to more dissatisfaction.

In trying to lessen the gloominess of these realties—or escape them altogether—men and women rush down numerous pathways to find happiness that will not fade away.

The sensualists find booze, drugs, and sex. The aesthetes shut out the world and revel in their art, décor, and other luxuries. Others devote themselves to gaining riches, power, and/or fame. Still others find solace and relief in religion and religious traditions.

These people often appear to find happiness. Their souls are lulled into a sweet, intoxicating state of forgetfulness. They have escaped evil...or so it seems. Then the day of misfortune comes, and their happiness is shredded because their soul is unprepared.

Over every person's joy and good times hangs the executioner's ax of pain, ready at any moment to destroy the soul of those who are unprotected by knowledge.

Consider the child crying to become a man or a woman. The man and woman long for the carefree days of childhood. The poor person is frustrated by the chains of poverty. The rich person worries about becoming poor or travels the world searching for elusive happiness.

Sometimes, a person feels that they have found true happiness by adopting a certain religion or by embracing an intellectual philosophy. Then some overpowering temptation proves the religion to be not enough or the philosophy is found to be a useless prop...

Is there no way to escape this terrible pain and sorrow that waits? Is there no way to get out of the chains of evil that already hold me tight? Are constant peace and happiness just a foolish dream?

THE GREAT ESCAPE

Peace and happiness are not just a pipe dream. There is a path to permanent prosperity and peace, free from worry and fear!

The first step is to understand the nature of evil. You can't just deny or ignore evil; it must be understood. You can't just pray for God to remove the evil; you need to find out why the evil is there and what you are supposed to learn from it in your life.

There is no point in complaining and worrying about the negative circumstances in your life that keep you down. You have to figure out *why* and *how* they keep you down. The way to do this is to get outside yourself and examine and understand yourself.

You have to stop resisting and fighting in the school of experience. Instead, calm yourself and be patient and begin to learn the lessons that are being taught through the negatives in your life. Evil—once you understand it—will become nothing but a passing experience. It has no superpowers over you. It can't keep you from your dreams of peace and happiness unless you give it that power.

THE EVIL TEACHER

When you see it this way, evil becomes a teacher to those who are willing to learn. It's not some mysterious and random outside force; instead, it's an experience inside your own heart. If you are patient and examine your heart, you will understand where the evil came from and why it's there.

"Evil becomes a teacher to those who are willing to learn."

This discovery will mean that you can free yourself of the evil by your own power and will. All evil is meant to instruct and is never permanent. It takes root when a person is ignorant of the nature and relation of things.

As long as you remain ignorant, you will remain the prisoner of negativity. Evil in the universe is a result of ignorance. If we were ready to learn from it, we would, as a species, be led to a higher wisdom and watch the evil vanish away. But mankind is not ready or willing to learn such lessons, and so we remain in evil.

THE BURNING BOY

Back in the day, before electricity in households was commonplace...

There was a boy who would cry to play with the candle when his mother would take him to bed. Every night he would do this. One night, his mother was tired and let her guard down. The boy grabbed the candle and was burned. He never wanted to play with the candle again. By this one foolish act, the boy learned well the lesson of obedience. And he also learned that fire burns.

This story is a thorough illustration of the nature, meaning, and result of evil.

The child was burned because of his ignorance of the nature of fire. Men and women likewise suffer through their ignorance of the nature of the things for which they strive. When they secure these things, they are harmed.

LURKING IN THE SHADOWS

Evil has always been symbolized by darkness and good by light. Within this symbolism is a great interpretation of reality: light floods the earth; darkness is just a shadow cast by a small body that is intercepting a few rays of the light. Similarly, the Supreme Good is the positive, life-giving power, and evil is the small shadow cast by self that shuts off the bright rays of light from entering the soul.

The darkness of night covers only half our planet, while the whole universe is ablaze with light. Every person knows that they will wake up to the light of morning.

Remember this when sadness and pain come to you and you stumble along unsure of where to go: You are intercepting the light of your own personal goals and desires. The dark shadow that covers you is cast by no one and nothing but yourself.

Just as the darkness in the earth is just a shadow, an unreality with no permanent residence, so is the darkness you feel within. It is just a shadow passing over your evolving and light-bearing soul.

Darkness is temporary.

"The darkness you feel within is just a temporary shadow passing over you—cast by no one and nothing but yourself."

THROUGH THE DARKNESS

By passing through the darkness, you will understand good and evil. And you will be able to appreciate the light. And when the lessons of evil are learned, ignorance passes away and wisdom takes its place.

It is possible to refuse to learn these lessons and instead remain in the darkness. There you will deal with recurring disappointment, sadness, and frustration.

If you want to be free of the negativity that surrounds you, you have to want to learn. You have to go through the disciplinary process. Until you learn from the bad, you will not be able to gain wisdom, happiness, or peace.

Some might argue and deny the existence of such happiness and peace. They shut themselves in a dark room and say that there is no light. But outside, the light is everywhere and the darkness is only in their little room.

LET THERE BE LIGHT!

You can either shut out the light of truth or you can begin to smash the walls of cynicism and error. When you break down these walls that you have built around yourself, you will let in the glorious light.

Take time for self-reflection and self-examination. Try to realize that evil is just a passing phase. It is a shadow created by you. All your troubles have come to you by a process of absolute and perfect law. They have come to you because you require them. After enduring them and understanding them, you will be made stronger, wiser, and nobler.

When you have endured and gained this understanding, you will be in a position to create your own life—your own circumstances. You will be able to change evil into good and to write with a master-hand the story of your destiny.

REFLECT

- Bad things are going to happen to you. This is an unavoidable fact of life.
- You can't escape evil forever—power, money, booze, drugs, and even religion won't last.
- You can prepare yourself and be ready for the bad times.

Here's how…

- Understand evil/negativity in your life. Don't deny or ignore it.
- Don't worry or complain.
- Figure out why the evil is in your life and how it's negatively affecting your life.
- Don't resist the school of experience—learn your lessons.

Remember…

- Evil can be just a passing experience. It only has the power you give it.
- Negativity stays in our life because of our own ignorance.

- Things we strive for often end up hurting us.
- Darkness is just a shadow—don't live in the darkness of your own shadow.
- We have to go through bad times to fully understand and appreciate the good.
- The light (the good) is inside and all around you.
- You can examine your own life and learn and grow from the negativity within.

After this, you will be able to begin creating the life that you want for yourself!

DISCUSS

What are some negatives in your life right now?

Are you leaning on something other than yourself to bring you comfort and happiness?

Do you find yourself worrying or complaining about circumstances in your life?

What can you learn from the negative circumstances in your life?

What kind of life would you like to live?

What do you want people to say about you when you're dead?

CHAPTER 2

THE WORLD IS A REFLEX OF MENTAL STATES

"You are what you think."

—BUDDHA

WHAT YOU ARE

Your world is what you are.

Everything in the universe is filtered through your inward experience. It doesn't really matter much what is outside because it is all a reflection of your own state of mind. What matters is what's inside, because that will dictate what you see outside.

Everything that you know for sure is held within your own experience. Everything that you *will* know must pass through the gateway of experience and then become part of yourself.

Your thoughts, desires, and aspirations make up your world. All that you see in the universe, whether it is beauty and happiness or ugliness and pain, is within yourself. You ruin or build your world, your universe, by your own thoughts.

"All that you see in the universe is within yourself."

Whatever you think and build within yourself will be shown in your outward circumstances. Your outside life molds itself to your inner thoughts and desires. This is the law of reaction.

The person who is selfish and greedy is heading toward misfortune and catastrophe. The person who is unselfish and noble is heading toward happiness and prosperity. Every person attracts his or her own experiences, and nothing can possibly come to that individual that does not belong to him or her. This is the universality of Divine law.

The incidents of every human life are drawn to them by their own inner thoughts. Each person is a complex combination of thoughts and experiences. The body is just a vehicle that shows these thoughts and experiences. In other words, you are what your thoughts are, and the world around you is clothed in your thoughts.

Buddha says, "All that we are is the result of what we have thought; it is founded on our thoughts; it is made up of our thoughts."

If a person is happy, it is because they think happy thoughts. If they are miserable, it is because they think depressing and negative thoughts.

Whether a person is fearful or fearless, foolish or wise, troubled or calm, it is always because of what they think inside, never what happens on the outside.

Do outside circumstances not affect our minds? What about natural disasters, tragic death, murder, and mayhem?

THINGS THAT HAPPEN

Circumstances can affect you only as long or as much as you let them do so.

You are influenced by circumstances because you don't understand the use and power of thought. You believe (and on this word *belief* hang all our joys and sorrows) that outside forces have the power to build or ruin your life.

By these thoughts (which become belief), you have become a slave to outside circumstances, whatever they are. Now you have given them a power that, in reality and by themselves, they do not have. Then you surrender, *not to the circumstances themselves*, but to the gloom or gladness, weakness or strength, fear or hope, with which your thoughts have clothed the circumstances.

TWO GUYS, NO MONEY

Two young men each lost their life savings. They had worked hard for years to save this money and lost it all in one fell swoop.

After hearing the news of complete loss, the first man was deeply troubled, stressed out, and depressed. He went straight to the liquor store. He bought a few bottles of whiskey and began to drink in an effort to lessen the negative thoughts and feelings within himself.

The second man read in his morning newspaper about the hopeless failure of the bank in which his money was deposited. He, too, had lost all. He remarked, "Well, it's gone, and trouble and worry won't bring it back, but hard work will." He dug himself into his work with a renewed energy and rapidly became prosperous.

The first man continued drinking and complaining about his "bad luck." Adverse circumstances continued to beat him around. He had become a slave to his negative thoughts.

The loss of money was a curse to the first man because he immediately clothed the event with dark and dreary thoughts. The loss became a blessing to the second man because he clothed the event with thoughts of strength, hope, and renewed efforts.

If life was truly just a result of external circumstances, then these two men would have been blessed or cursed in the same way. But the young men's different outcomes prove that thoughts about and reactions to circumstances are far more important than the circumstances themselves.

When you realize this truth, you will begin to control your thoughts. You will begin to discipline your mind and treat your soul as a valuable temple. Eliminate all useless and negative thinking, and fill your mind with thoughts of strength, calmness, love, and beauty. Do this and you will become strong, calm, loving, and beautiful.

THINGS WE SEE

Just as we surround outside events with thoughts of our own choosing, so also do we clothe objects in the visible world with whatever thoughts we select. Where one person sees harmony and beauty, another sees revolting ugliness.

An enthusiastic botanist was walking along a country lane when she came to a puddle of brackish water near a farmyard. She bent down and filled a bottle full of the water so she could later examine it under a microscope.

The teenage son of the farmer sauntered up and leaned against the fence nearby. The botanist, noticing the young man, began to speak excitedly and at great length about the hidden and innumerable specimens contained in the water. She concluded by saying, "Yes, there is a hundred—no, a million—universes contained within this pool, had we the sense or the instruments to catch and examine them."

The young man spit tobacco juice on the ground and said, "Hell, there's a lotta tadpoles in there, but they're easy to catch."

The botanist, her mind full of the knowledge of natural facts, saw beauty, harmony, and hidden wonders in the water. The farmer's son, his mind empty of such facts and thoughts, saw only a mud puddle.

The wildflower, which the casual passerby tramples unnoticed, is to the poet an angelic messenger from the invisible. To many people, the ocean is a dreary expanse of water on which ships sail and sometimes wreck. To the soul of the musician, it is a living thing, and he or she hears divine harmonies in its changing moods.

Where the ordinary mind sees disaster and confusion, the mind of the philosopher sees the perfect sequence of cause and effect. The materialist sees nothing but endless death where the mystic sees exciting and eternal life.

PEOPLE WE MEET

We dress events and objects in whatever thoughts we choose, and we do the same with people.

The suspicious believe everybody to be suspicious. The liar doesn't believe that anyone always tells the truth. The jealous see jealousy in every person. The miser thinks that everyone is out to get his or her money.

The man who ignores his own conscience in his quest for wealth sleeps with a pistol under his pillow, assured that the world is full of careless people looking to rob him. The abandoned sensualist, characterized by drinking, drugs, and sex, believes the saint is a hypocrite.

Those who think loving thoughts see in others reasons to love and sympathize. The trusting and honest are not bothered with suspicions. The good-natured and generous are happy for the good fortune of others. The person who sees the Divine in themselves will recognize it in all beings, even in the animals.

"The person who sees the Divine in themselves will recognize it in all beings."

Men and women are unlikely to change this mental outlook because they attract people similar to themselves—by the law of cause and effect.

The old saying "Birds of a feather flock together" has a deeper meaning than is usually attached to it. Not just in the physical world, but also in thoughts and mentality, each person clings to its kind.

A POEM

Do you wish for kindness? Be kind.
Do you ask for truth? Be true.
What you give of yourself you find;
Your world is a reflex of you.

HEAVEN WITHIN

If you are one who is waiting for heaven or an afterlife to experience happiness, here is good news for you: You many enter into that happy world right now. It is within you, waiting for you to find and possess it.

A wise person who knew the inner laws of being once said, "When men say, 'Look here!' or 'Look there,' do not go after them; the kingdom of God is within you."

What you have to do is believe this; believe it without doubt in your mind. Then think about it; meditate upon it until you understand it. You will then begin to clean out and rebuild your inner world. As you experience revelations and realizations, you will discover the helplessness of outward circumstances against the magic power of a self-controlled soul.

ANOTHER POEM

If you want to right the world,
And banish all the evils and its woes,
Make its wild places bloom,
And its dreary deserts blossom as the rose,—
Then right yourself.

If you want to turn the world,
From its long captivity in sin,
Restore all broken hearts,
Slay grief, and let sweet consolation in,—
Then turn yourself.

If you want to cure the world
Of its long sickness, end its grief and pain;
Bring in all-healing Joy,
And give to the afflicted rest again,—
Then cure yourself.

If you want to wake the world
Out of its dream of death and darkening strife
Bring it to Love and Peace,
And light and brightness of immortal life,—
Then wake yourself.

REFLECT

- Your world is a reflection of you.
- Your thoughts make up your outward life and circumstances.

With that in mind…

- Eliminate useless and negative thoughts.
- Things that happen can affect you only in the way that you let them.
- People you meet appear the way you perceive them to be—according to your thoughts.
- You are attracted to and attract people with similar thoughts as yourself.
- The things we see are colored and described by our thoughts.

Good news…

- Heaven is inside you.
- Whatever you wish to change in the world first change in yourself.

DISCUSS

Are you happy with your life?

What do you think about?

Do you often dwell on negative thoughts?

How would you describe your friends—the people you hang around?

Do you see things in the world as generally negative or positive?

What about people—do you see them in a generally positive or negative light?

Are you waiting until death to enter heaven?

What would you like to change in the world?

Can you change that same thing within yourself?

CHAPTER 3

THE WAY OUT OF UNDESIRABLE CONDITIONS

"Circumstances are the rulers of the weak; they are but the instruments of the wise."

—SAMUEL LOVER

UNDERSTANDING THE LAW

Now you realize the true nature of evil. It's a passing shadow thrown by you that temporarily blocks the light of the supreme and eternal good.

You also realize that the world is a mirror in which each person sees a reflection of himself or herself.

We can now ascend, with confident and easy steps, to that level of perception where we can see and realize the vision of the Law.

With this realization comes the knowledge that everything is in an endless cycle of cause and effect. Nothing can be separated from this law. From the most meaningless thought or act of a human being to the constellations of the stars, law reigns supreme.

No random condition can exist even for a minute. If it did, then the law would be denied and annihilated. Every condition of life is arranged into an orderly and harmonious sequence. And the secret and origin of every condition is contained within itself.

The law, "Whatsoever a man sows that shall he also reap," is inscribed in flaming letters upon the doorway to eternity. No one can deny it, no one can cheat it, and no one can escape it. He who puts his hand in the fire will be burned until he removes it. Neither curses nor prayers can change this. The same law governs the mind.

Hatred, anger, jealousy, lust, and covetousness are all fires that burn. Whoever entertains these conditions will suffer the torments of burning within. All these conditions of the mind are called "evil" because they are subconscious efforts of the soul to overthrow the law. They lead to chaos and confusion within. Sooner or later, they are shown in outward

"The law, 'Whatsoever a man sows that shall he also reap,' is inscribed in flaming letters upon the doorway to eternity. No one can deny it, no one can cheat it, and no one can escape it."

circumstances as disease, failure, misfortune, grief, pain, and depression.

Love, gentleness, goodwill, and purity are cooling airs that breathe peace upon the soul that seeks them. They are in harmony with the eternal law and become actualized in the form of health, peaceful surroundings, and undeviating success and good fortune.

A sound understanding of this great law of the universe leads to the gain of that state of mind known as obedience—obedience to the law. Justice, harmony, and love are supreme in the universe, and all adverse and painful conditions are the result of our disobedience to that law. This knowledge leads to strength and power. A life of true happiness and success can be built upon this knowledge alone.

If you will be patient under all circumstances and accept them as necessary to your training, you will rise superior to all painful conditions. You will overcome them with a power that is certain and leaves no fear of their return. By the power of obedience, they are slain.

Those working in harmony with the law have, in fact, identified themselves with the law. Whatever those individuals conquer they conquer forever; whatever they build can't be destroyed.

THE POWER INSIDE

The cause of all power and weakness is within. The secret to all happiness and misery is within.

There is no personal progress without looking inside. And there is no sure gain of prosperity or peace without an intentional development of knowledge.

You say you are chained by circumstances; you cry out for better opportunities, more control, and better physical conditions. Inside, maybe you curse the hand that holds you down.

It is for you that I write.

It is to you that I speak.

Listen, and let my words burn themselves into your heart. What I say is the truth:

If you will commit to improving your inner life, you can create the outward life that you want.

I know this path looks uninteresting at first. The truth always does; only error and delusion look inviting and fascinating at first. But if you decide to go down this road, discipline your mind, get rid of your weaknesses, and allow your soul-forces and spiritual powers to reveal themselves, you will be amazed at the magical changes that happen in your life.

As you go on, golden opportunities will be thrown across your path. And the wisdom to use them properly will spring up within you. Good friends will come to you without being sought. Similar people will be drawn to you like the needle to the magnet, and all necessary resources will be provided to you.

Maybe you are poor, alone, and feel as though you have no friends. You wish that your life were better, but it seems to get worse at every turn. You feel as though a dark cloud follows you wherever you go.

Maybe you complain about your situation. Maybe you blame your parents or your employer. Maybe you blame the powers that be for dealing you a bad hand in life while someone else you know seems to have so much going for them. You think it's not fair that you should have so little while they have so much.

Stop complaining and stop worrying.

None of the people or things that you blame for your problems is the reason.

You are the reason.

The cause of your bad situation is inside you. And where the cause is, there is the remedy. The fact that you are a complainer shows that you deserve your poor circumstances. You lack faith, and that is the basis of all effort and progress.

There is no place for a complainer in the universe of law. Worrying is suicide of the soul. By these attitudes, you are strengthening the negativity that chains you down and increasing the darkness that surrounds you.

Change your outlook on life, and your outward life will change. Build yourself up inside by faith and knowledge and make yourself worthy of better circumstances and better opportunities. Be sure that you are making the best of what you have.

MAKE GOOD OUT OF BAD

Don't think that you can step into greater situations and advantages while overlooking the smaller ones that you already have. If you could, the greater situation would be temporary, and you would fall back into your prior situation to learn the lessons you had neglected.

This can be seen in 70 percent of lottery winners. The majority of lottery winners end up broke or worse within a few years of winning the lottery. Why?

Because they didn't use the money they had *before* winning millions wisely. When they won millions, they didn't suddenly become good with money. They were not ready to deal with the responsibility and pressures that would come with winning all that money.

In school, one must complete the first lesson before passing on to the next. So it is in life. Before you can have the greater life that you desire, you have to understand and use fully what you already have.

If we misuse or neglect what we already have—even if we have only a little—then it will be taken from us because we have shown that we are unworthy of it.

Maybe you live in a little apartment in a dangerous location and are surrounded by crime and other bad influences. You want to move out to a cleaner, more prosperous neighborhood and house. If so, first take care of the place you live in now. Make it as clean as possible.

Do the best you can in preparing your meager meals. Make the place look nice. Be welcoming and kind. Smile often.

By elevating your present circumstances, you will rise above them. And you will rise above the need of them. At the right time, you will move into the better house and surroundings that have been waiting for you.

"By elevating your present circumstances, you will rise above them."

Maybe you want more time for thought or your own work. You feel that you don't have enough time due to the hours of labor you are working for a paycheck. If so, then make sure you are using what little spare time you have to the fullest.

It's useless to want more time when you're wasting what little free time you have. More time would only make you lazier and more indifferent.

Even poverty and lack of time are not the curse that you might think they are. If they prevent your happiness, it is because you have clothed them in your own weaknesses, and the evil that you see in them is really in yourself.

Try to understand and realize that as you shape and build your mind, you are the builder of your destiny. By the power of your increasing self-discipline, you will see that these so-called evils can be changed into blessings.

You can use your poverty to develop patience, hope, and courage. You can use your lack of time to develop punctual habits, prompt decision-making, and precise use of time.

In poor soil, some of the most beautiful flowers have grown. In poverty, some of the best individuals have developed. Where there are difficulties and uncomfortable conditions, goodness and advantages grow strong.

Maybe your boss is an evil tyrant and treats you harshly. Look at this as necessary to your training. Return his unkindness with gentleness and forgiveness. Practice constant patience and self-control. Turn the disadvantage into an advantage by gaining spiritual and mental strength.

By your silent example, you will be a teacher to the boss, and he will grow ashamed of his behavior. At the same time, you will be lifting yourself up to be ready for the opportunity to step into a better situation when it presents itself.

SLAVERY

Do not complain about being a slave. Behave in such a way that lifts you above the plane of slavery. Before you complain about being a slave to another, make sure you are not a slave to self.

Look inside, honestly, and pull no punches. You might find slavish thoughts, slavish desires, and slavish habits in your daily life. If you conquer these, you will no longer be a slave to self. Stop being a slave to self, and no man will have the power to enslave you.

When you are able to overcome self, you will overcome all challenges, and difficulties will fall before you.

Don't complain that you are oppressed by the rich. Are you sure that if you became rich that you would not be an oppressor yourself?

Remember that the eternal law is justice, and he who is cruel today will be treated cruelly tomorrow. From this law there is no escape.

Maybe in a former life, you were rich and an oppressor, and now you are paying off the debt that you owe the great law. Meditate on faith, strength, and the eternal good.

Try to lift yourself above the personal and temporary into the impersonal and permanent. Forget the idea that you are being picked on or singled out unjustly by another. Instead, realize a deeper comprehension of your inner life. You are injured only by what is within you.

"You are injured only by what is within you."

There is no habit more degrading and soul-destroying than self-pity. Get rid of this habit as soon as possible. It is a canker sore that is feeding upon your heart, and it is preventing you from gaining a better life.

Stop judging others and stop judging yourself.

Don't allow yourself thoughts and desires that are not pure and good. By paying attention to these things, you will build yourself a permanent foundation, and all that is needed for your happiness and well-being will come to you in its own time.

There is no way to permanently get out of poverty or any negative condition without getting rid of selfishness and negativity within.

TRUE RICHES AND PROSPERITY

The way to true riches is to enrich the soul with moral goodness. Outside of heart-virtue, there is neither prosperity nor power, but only the appearances of these.

Some people make money and have no measure of virtue, but such money is not true riches. Its possession is temporary and emotional.

The rich man who is without virtue is, in reality, poor. In the middle of his riches, he is drifting toward poverty. Even if he becomes rich many times, he must continually be thrown back into poverty until he conquers the poverty within.

But the man who is poor on the outside and has much virtue within is truly rich. In the middle of his poverty, he is traveling toward prosperity. Happiness and bliss wait for him.

If you want to become truly and permanently prosperous, you must first become virtuous. It is unwise to aim directly at prosperity, to make it the one object of life, to reach out greedily for it. This will ultimately defeat you. Instead, aim for self-perfection; make service the object of your life. Reach out for the supreme good.

MOTIVES FOR MONEY

You say you want wealth in order to do good with it and to help others. If this is your true motive in wanting wealth, then wealth will come to you. You are strong and unselfish if, in the middle of riches, you can look at yourself as a steward and not as an owner.

But examine your motives. Many times, when money is desired for the object of helping others, the real motive is a love of popularity and the desire to pose as a philanthropist or reformer.

If you are not helping others with what little bit you have, then more money would only make you more selfish. If you appeared to do good with your money, it would be for self-praise.

If your real desire is to do good, you don't need to wait for money to do it. Do it now, this moment, just where you are. If you are as unselfish, as you believe yourself to be, you will show it by sacrificing yourself for others now. No matter how poor you are, there is room for self-sacrifice.

The person who truly desires to do good does not wait for money before doing it, but sacrifices self and helps neighbor and stranger, friend and enemy, alike.

Cause and effect: inner good becomes prosperity and power; inner evil becomes poverty and weakness.

Money does not make up true wealth. Position does not make up power, and to rely on these things alone is to stand on a slippery place. Your true wealth is in your heart's virtue, and true power is the way in which you use it.

Correct your heart, and you will correct your life. Lust, hatred, anger, vanity, pride, covetousness, self-indulgence, self-seeking, obstinacy—these are poverty and weakness.

Love, purity, gentleness, meekness, patience, compassion, generosity, self-forgetfulness, and self-renunciation—these are wealth and power.

As you conquer your heart, an irresistible and all-conquering power is evolved from within. If you establish yourself in the highest virtue, the world will fall at your feet.

The rich sometimes are more unhappy than the poor. How we see that happiness depends on the inward life, not the outward possessions.

EMPLOYER/EMPLOYEE RELATIONS

Perhaps you are an employer, and you have endless troubles with your employees. When you hire good and faithful people, they quickly leave you. As a result, you are losing, or have lost, your faith in human nature.

Maybe you try to fix things by increasing wages and being more lenient. Still things remain the same.

Allow me to offer some advice.

The secret of your troubles is not in your employees; it is in you. If you look inside with a sincere desire to discover and get rid of your error, you will—sooner or later—find the cause of your problems.

It may be some selfish desire, or suspicions, or an unkind attitude that sends out poison among your employees—even though it might be unnoticeable in your behavior and speech. Think of your workers with kindness; think about their happiness and comfort. Never expect them to do anything that you would not care to do if you were in their position.

It's rare to find employees who forget themselves for the good of the employer. Rarer still is the employer who wants happiness for his employees more than for himself. This person's happiness increases immensely, and he doesn't need to complain about his employees.

One well-known employer of labor says, "I have always had good relations with my workers. If you ask me how, I can only say that it is my goal to do them as I would wish to be done."

That is the secret to gaining positive employer/ employee relations and the secret to overcoming those conditions that are currently negative.

LONELINESS

Maybe you are lonely and "don't have a friend in the world." Blame nobody but yourself. Be friendly toward others, and friends will soon flock around you. Make yourself pure and lovable, and you will be loved by all.

Any conditions that you find negative in your life you can get out of by disciplining your mind and yourself. Whether it's poverty, misfortunes, griefs, or annoyances that form the dark cloud over your head, you may be free of this negativity by overcoming the selfish elements inside you that give them life.

It doesn't matter that there are past acts and thoughts that must be worked out and possibly forgiven. Right now, we have fresh thoughts and actions and the power to make them good or bad. Nor does it mean that if we (reaping what we have sown) have to lose money or position, that we also lose our strength and standards. It is in these things that our wealth, power, and happiness are found.

The person who holds on to self is his or her own enemy and sees enemies all around. The person who lets go of self becomes his or her own savior and is surrounded by friends. Come out of your poverty and pain by coming out of yourself.

"Come out of your poverty and pain by coming out of yourself."

Let the petty selfishness fall from you and try on universal love. You will then realize inward heaven, and it will be reflected in your outward life.

If you can conquer yourself, you will find the highest prosperity and lasting joy and bliss.

REFLECT

- If you will commit to improving your inner life, you can create the outward life that you want.

Natural law is absolute…

- The universe operates on an endless cycle of cause and effect.
- The same law that governs the universe governs the mind.
- Negative thoughts lead to negative circumstances, positive thoughts to positive circumstances.
- Understand this law and train your mind accordingly.

For this reason, let these guidelines govern your thoughts and actions…

- Stop complaining, blaming, and worrying. *You* are the reason for your problems.
- Do the best you can with what you have right now.
- Keep a positive attitude regardless of your circumstances.
- Use bad situations to develop good habits and skills (e.g., money management, time management, discipline, etc.).

- Don't ask for more (e.g., time, money, etc.) until you become a good steward of what you already have.
- Stop being a slave to self; rid yourself of bad habits, desires, and thoughts.
- Don't judge others.
- Question your motives.
- Overcome your selfishness and good things will come your way.

DISCUSS

Do you dedicate most of your thoughts to negative emotions?

Do you complain about your job, your car, your spouse, your boss, etc.?

Are you doing the best you can with what you have?

If you feel like you don't have enough money, can you think of ways to spend less so that you have more?

If you feel like you don't have enough time, can you think of ways to increase efficiency and manage your time more effectively?

Have you ever tried to consciously maintain a positive attitude—no matter what?

Are there negative habits in your life that cost you money, health, and positive energy?

Do you criticize other people to feel better about yourself?

Whom do you blame for the negatives in your life?

CHAPTER 4

THE SILENT POWER OF THOUGHT

> *"The significant problems we face in life cannot be solved at the same level of thinking we were at when we created them."*
>
> —ALBERT EINSTEIN

The most powerful forces in the universe are silent.

According to their intensity, forces become beneficial when rightly directed and destructive when wrongly used. This is common knowledge regarding mechanical forces such as steam, electricity, etc. But few have learned to apply this knowledge to the mind, where thought-forces are constantly being created and sent forth as salvation or destruction.

Mental forces are the most powerful of all.

At this stage in our evolution, humans have controlled these forces and the result is our present trend of advancement. All the wisdom available on earth can be found only in complete self-mastery.

"All wisdom can be found only in complete self-mastery."

The command "Love your enemies" is urgent advice to take advantage of that wisdom by mastering your mind. Most people are slaves to their mind, floating like a straw on the stream of selfishness.

The Hebrew prophets always related outward events to inward thought. They associated national disasters and successes with the thoughts and desires that dominated the nation at the time.

The knowledge of causal power of thought is the basis of all real wisdom and power.

National events are the manifestation of the psychic forces of the nation. Wars, plagues, and famines are the meeting and clashing of wrongly directed thought-forces. It is foolish to ascribe war to the influence of one person or to one body of people. It is the crowning horror of national selfishness.

IT ALL STARTS WITH A THOUGHT

Silent thought-forces bring everything we see into existence.

Matter is merely objectified thought.

All of mankind's achievements began in thought. The author, the inventor, and the architect first build their work in their mind. Once they have completed it mentally, then they begin to materialize their work in the form of book, machine, or building.

When thought-forces are in harmony with the overruling law, they are uplifting and protecting, but when disruptive, they become destructive.

Adjust your thoughts to a complete faith in the supremacy of good. Realize that within you is the solution and destruction of all evil.

Believe and ye shall live.

This is the true meaning of salvation. Enter into the living light of good and find salvation from darkness and negativity.

Fear, worry, anxiety, doubt, trouble, chagrin, and disappointment come from ignorance and a lack of faith. These mental conditions are the result of selfishness. They are based on an inherent belief in the supremacy of evil.

Humanity needs salvation from these conditions, and no man or woman can talk of salvation when they are a slave to such mental troubles. To fear, to worry, and to doubt is to disbelieve in good.

Weakness and failure emerge from these states of mind, because they represent the destruction of the positive thought-forces that would have resulted in benefits.

When you overcome these negative thoughts, you will enter into a life of power. You will cease to be a slave, and you will become a master.

Negative thoughts can be overcome by steady and persistent growth in inward knowledge.

To mentally deny evil is not enough; it must be understood on a daily basis and then transcended. To mentally affirm the good is not enough; it must be understood and entered into.

The practice of self-control leads to a knowledge of one's thought-forces. Later, it leads to the power by which they are used correctly and for good.

If you can master self and your mental forces, then you can master your affairs and outward circumstances. If everything goes wrong for a person, it is because they dwell in negative thoughts.

If you constantly wallow in doubt, fear, or worry, then you are a slave. And you will remain a slave even though success may be knocking at your door. You lack faith and do not control your life, and as a result, you are a slave to circumstances—and to yourself.

Still you can learn from this negativity and ultimately become strong through the lessons of bitter experience.

Faith and purpose are the motive-power of life. There is nothing you can't accomplish with a strong faith and an unflinching purpose. Exercise faith daily, and your thought-forces will be gathered together. Strengthen your purpose daily, and those forces will be directed toward achieving that purpose.

Whatever your position in life may be, you must learn how to cultivate calm and tranquility. When you are able to do this, you can focus your thought-forces on your purpose.

Maybe you are a business person, and you are suddenly confronted with some overwhelming difficulty or probable disaster. You are anxious and stressed out and at your wits' end. To remain in this state of mind is fatal, for when anxiety steps in, correct judgment steps out.

"Negative thoughts can be overcome by steady and persistent growth in inward knowledge."

A CALM MIND

Instead, take advantage of a quiet hour or two in the early morning or at night. Go somewhere you will be free from interruption. Force yourself to think of something positive and not the situation that is causing the stress. Eventually, a calm strength will flow into your mind and your stress will pass away.

When you feel your mind wandering back to the stress, bring it back to the peaceful spot again. When you've done this, you can then concentrate your whole mind on solving your problem. What you originally saw as a nightmare during your stress now becomes a problem easily solved with clarity and calmness of mind and judgment.

Clear vision and perfect judgment belong only to a calm and untroubled mind. When the proper course of action presents itself, carry it out.

It might take daily practice to get to the point where you are able to calm the mind on demand. If you keep working at it, you will persevere.

When you get back into the daily grind, it is likely that worries will creep back into your mind. Do not respond. Be guided only by the vision of calmness and not the shadows of anxiety. The hour of calmness is the hour of illumination and correct judgment.

By calming the mind, you are channeling all your scattered thought-forces into one powerful ray of thought. This brings far more power to a problem than does a worried mind.

There is no difficulty, however great, that will not yield before a calm and powerful concentration of thought.

Once you have gone deeply into your inner nature, and have overcome many enemies that lurk there, you can begin to understand the subtle power of thought. You will also see its inseparable relation to outward and material things and its magical potency in transforming the conditions of life.

THOUGHTS AS ENERGY FORCES

Every thought you think is a force sent out. According to its nature and intensity, it will go out and sink into the minds receptive to it and will react for good or evil. There is a constant reciprocity between mind and mind and a continual interchange of thought-forces.

Selfish and disturbing thoughts are destructive forces. They are messengers of evil sent out to stimulate and add to the evil in other minds. Those other minds send them back to you with added destructive power.

Thoughts that are calm and unselfish are like angelic messengers sent out into the world with healing powers. They counteract the evil forces and pour the oil of joy on the waters of anxiety. They restore broken hearts.

Think good thoughts, and they will quickly materialize in your outward life in the form of good conditions. Control your thought-forces and you will be able to shape your outward life as you want.

MIND CONTROL

The difference between a savior and a sinner is this: the one has a perfect control of all the forces within him; the other is dominated and controlled by them.

There is no other way to true power and peace except by self-control. If you are at the mercy of your moods, you'll be unhappy and of little real use in the world. You have to conquer all of your petty likes and dislikes, your capricious loves and hates, your fits of anger, suspicion, jealousy, and all your changing moods.

This is the only way to create a life of happiness and prosperity.

When you are enslaved by your changing moods, you will need to depend on others and outward aides as you walk through life. If you want to walk with confidence and independence, you have to learn to rise above such disturbances of the mind.

Practice "going into silence" every day. This is putting your mind at rest. It is the method of replacing a troubled thought with one of peace, a thought of weakness with one of strength.

After you become successful at this practice, you will be able to direct your mental forces toward the problems and pursuits of life.

When you acquire calmness and control and direct the thought currents within your mind, you will save your soul and cultivate your heart and life.

"The universe helps those who control their lives."

THE RISE OF POWER

As you succeed in gaining control over your impulses, moods, and thoughts, you will begin to feel, growing within you, a new and silent power. A settled feeling of composure and strength will remain with you. Your powers will begin to show themselves.

In areas where you used to be weak and ineffectual, you will now be able to be strong. You will be able to work with a calm confidence that commands success.

Along with this new power and strength you will find "intuition." Your mind will be illuminated, and you will see clearly and with certainty.

Judgment and mental acuity will increase. You will be able to sense coming events and to forecast, with great accuracy, the result of your efforts.

Your outlook on life will change, and others' attitudes toward you will change. As you rise above the destructive thought-forces, you will come into positive, strong currents of thought. Your happiness will increase, and you will begin to realize the joy, strength, and power that come only from self-mastery.

This strength and happiness and power will constantly be radiating from you. You will attract other strong people to you without even trying. Influence will put into your hands. And of course, your outward circumstances will conform to your new thought-world.

Your enemies are internal. If you want to be happy and strong, you have to stop allowing negative streams of thought into your mind.

You must learn to command and control your desires—and to decide with authority what thoughts we will allow into the mansion of our soul. Even small successes in this area will add much power to one's life.

If you are able to master this control of mind, you will find undreamed-of wisdom, inner strength, and peace. You will realize that the universe helps those who control their lives.

REFLECT

- Thought is the most powerful force in the universe—the source of all creation, innovation, and achievement.
- Understanding the power of thought is the basis of all real wisdom and power.

Negative thoughts hold you back in life…

- Wars, plagues, famines, and other widespread ills are the result of collective, wrongly directed thought-forces.
- Fears, worries, and doubts are destructive forces.

- When you wallow in negativity, you become a slave to circumstance.
- Overcome negative thoughts, and you will become powerful.

So, learn to cultivate calmness and tranquility…

- Direct your scattered thoughts into one powerful ray of positive thought.
- Establish yourself on the path to power and peace through self-control.
- Master your moods and impulses, and you will master your fate.

DISCUSS

Do you send out destructive thought-forces by disliking, envying, or resenting someone?

Do you give up strength by holding on to bitter feelings and angry thoughts?

Do you believe that goodness is the most powerful force?

In what ways can you overcome negative thoughts?

Do you calm your mind before making important decisions?

Do you allow your mood to dictate what kind of day you will have?

How can you cultivate inner tranquility regardless of outward circumstance?

CHAPTER 5

THE SECRET OF HEALTH, SUCCESS, AND POWER

> *"The pleasantest things in the world are pleasant thoughts: and the great art of life is to have as many of them as possible."*
>
> —MONTAIGNE

THOUGHT-FAIRIES

We all remember fondly, as children, how we listened to fairy tales.

We followed the ever-changing fortunes of the good boy or girl. They were always protected in the hour of crisis from the scheming witch, the cruel giant, or the wicked hag. Our little hearts never lost confidence in our hero or heroine, and we knew they would defeat the villain in the end because the gods and the fairies would never desert those who were good and true.

What unspeakable joy flowed through us when the fairy-queen brought all her magic at the final moment, scattering all the darkness and trouble. The heroes were saved and were granted lives to live "happily ever after."

As we grew older and more acquainted with "reality," our fairy-tale world was destroyed. Its wonderful characters were shoved into the closet of the unreal, stored in the archives of our memory. We thought we were wise to dismiss forever the land of childish dreams.

But as we become little children again in the wonderful world of wisdom, we will return again to the inspiring dreams of childhood and find that they are realities after all.

The fairy-folk, so small and almost always invisible, possessed all-conquering magic power. They gave happiness, health, and wealth to the good. They become real again to the people who discover and take advantage of the power of thought. To these people, the fairies give thought-powers, while working in harmony with the supreme good. And these people, in reality, will gain true health, wealth, and happiness.

GOODNESS PROTECTS

There is no protection like goodness. And by "goodness" I don't mean simply conforming to society's rules of morality. I mean good thoughts, inspiration, unselfish love, and freedom from excessive pride.

If you dwell continually in good thoughts, you are essentially throwing a psychic atmosphere of sweetness and power around you that impresses all who come into contact with you.

The rising sun scares off the helpless shadows. A positive thought trumps the impotent forces of evil.

Where there is strong faith and goodness, there is success and power. Disease, failure, and disaster can't find lodging in such a place. There is nothing negative for them to feed upon.

Many people complain that they are worn out from working too hard. In the majority of these cases, the burnout comes from wasted energy. "Work smarter, not harder," as the saying goes. If you're stressed out or worried over needless details, you're inviting a breakdown.

Work—physical or mental—is beneficial. If you can work with a steady and calm persistency, you will accomplish much. A person whose mind is free of worry and stress can concentrate solely on the task at hand and will always get more done than the person who hurries and is anxious.

HAVE FAITH

Every lasting work is accomplished through the power of faith—faith in the supreme good, faith in the law, faith in your work, and faith in your power to get that work done. Faith is the rock upon which you build a life that will stand and not fall.

Under all circumstances, follow the highest promptings within you. Be true to yourself. Rely on your inward light and pursue your purpose with a fearless and peaceful heart. Believe that the future holds for you the reward of every thought and effort.

"Faith is the rock upon which you build a life that will stand and not fall."

Know that the laws of the universe never fail.

What you put out will come back to you with mathematical exactness. This is faith and the living of faith. By living this way, you will be able to navigate through the dark waters of doubt and difficulty. If you believe in your purpose and goals, you will pass through the rough times unharmed.

Do all you can to get this brand of faith; it is the ticket to all the happiness, success, peace, and power that make life great and so much better than slogging through in misery. Build a life that remains after death through this faith.

Whether you are thrown into hell's fury or lifted into the highest points of ecstasy, hold on tight to this faith. Come back and find solace in it. Keep your feet planted on its immortal base.

If you stay centered in such a strong faith, you will smash the forces of evil like a glass against the concrete. You will find success like the person with regular, half-hearted attempts can never know or imagine.

NO LUCK NECESSARY

There are plenty of men and women who have put this to the test. They live this faith day by day and have reaped the rewards of hanging on through the bad times. They have moved the mountains of sorrow and disappointment, of mental weariness and physical pain, and tossed them into the sea of oblivion.

Once you get a handle on this faith, you will no longer worry about future failure or success. You won't be nervous about results; you will work in happiness and peace, knowing that the right thoughts and efforts will bring the right results.

I know a lady who has succeeded in this way many times over. Recently, a friend remarked to her, "You are so lucky! You only have to wish for something and it comes to you!"

And, of course, this is how it appeared on the surface. But in reality, this lady worked through her life building and training herself for this success.

Mere wishing brings nothing but disappointment; it is living that tells. The foolish wish and grumble; the wise work and wait.

This woman worked on her outward and inward life, heart and soul. She built a life with the stones of faith, hope, joy, devotion, and love. The light radiated from her. It beamed in her eye and shone through her face. It vibrated in her voice, and all who came into contact with her felt its captivating spell.

And as with her, so with you…

GROW YOUR OWN LIFE

Your success, failure, and influence—your whole life—you carry with you. The dominant trends of your thoughts are the determining factors in your destiny.

Send out loving and happy thoughts, and good things will fall into your hands. Your table will be spread with the cloth of peace.

Send out hateful and selfish thoughts, and curses will rain down on you. Unrest and fear will wait on your pillow.

"The dominant trends of your thoughts are the determining factors in your destiny."

You are the unconditional maker of your fate, whether good or bad. Every minute you are sending out thought-forces that will make or break your life. Let your heart be large and loving and unselfish, and your influence will be powerful and lasting—regardless of how much money you make.

If you confine your thoughts to the narrow limits of self-interest, you could become a millionaire and still your influence and success will end up being insignificant.

So cultivate this unselfish spirit, combine it with faith and goodness, and focus on your purpose. From this you will grow health, success, greatness, and power.

BE PROACTIVE, BE PREPARED

Maybe you dislike your job, and your heart is not in your work. Still, do your best to work with care and precision while easing your mind with the idea that better work and greater opportunities are waiting for you. Then keep an active mental outlook for budding possibilities. Keep your resume up to date, fill out applications, make more connections.

When the critical moment of opportunity arrives, you will be ready to step in. Your mind will be prepared with the necessary intelligence that comes from mental discipline.

No matter what your current job is, throw yourself into it. Complete tasks, no matter how menial, the right way. These small undertakings lead to larger tasks. You will rise by steadily climbing.

Learn how to conserve your energies and resources so you can concentrate them—at any moment—on a single given point. It is foolish to waste all your mental and spiritual energy in frivolity, foolish chatter, selfish argument, or wasteful physical excesses.

LIKE A ROCK

If you want power, you need to grow calmness and silence inside.

You have to be able to stand alone.

Power and strength are associated with immovability. The mountain, the massive rock, the storm-tested oak all speak of power because they stand alone with a defiant permanence.

The shifting sand, the waving reed, and the yielding twig speak to us of weakness because they are movable and vulnerable to their environment.

A person of power is calm and unmoved when all others are swayed by some emotion or passion. Only someone with this inner stability is fit to command or control. Leaders must have control of themselves before they can lead others.

"Leaders must have control of themselves before they can lead others."

People that are hysterical, fearful, thoughtless, and frivolous will look for others to keep them company.

The calm and fearless will look for solitude in nature and draw power from this time alone. They will be more and more successful at navigating the psychic forces that surround human beings.

Passion is not power. Passion is like the storm that beats fiercely and wildly against the rock. Power is like the rock. It remains silent and unmoved throughout the storm.

Martin Luther put his life in danger when he traveled from Wittenberg to Worms to defend his beliefs. Some of his friends voiced their concern for his safety before he left. He responded by saying, "If there were as many devils in Worms as there are tiles on the housetops I would still go." This is an illustration of true power.

BE RELENTLESS!

Above all else, be of a single aim. Have a legitimate and useful purpose, and devote yourself to it. Don't let anything distract you. Remember that "the double-minded man is unstable in all his ways." Don't be unsure of yourself.

Be eager to learn, but slow to beg.

Understand your work, and make sure it is your own. Always follow your inner voice. You will progress step by step to victory, and your outlook will broaden. Soon you will see the life you've been dreaming of right before your eyes.

You will be in harmony with the great law, and you will find prosperity.

Unwavering faith, a wisely directed purpose, and the reigning in of desire are the keys to power.

REFLECT

- Have faith in the supreme good, which will return you to the magic of childhood.

When you dwell in good thoughts, you will…

- Exude sweetness and power.

- Conquer negativity.
- Accomplish significantly more.

Therefore, build your life upon faith and discover…

- How to stand alone.
- Stability amid uncertainty.
- Self-assurance in yourself and your purpose.

Remember, the dominant trends of your thoughts are the determining factors in your destiny!

DISCUSS

Do you find yourself overwhelmed at work?

Do stress and overwhelm prevent you from accomplishing as much as you would like?

Do you believe that you have the ability to get your work done?

Is it easier for you to grumble and wish than to work and wait?

Are you seeking out professional opportunities or allowing yourself to plateau?

Do you waste energy thinking of negative things?

Can you be alone and still be confident?

What's your purpose?

CHAPTER 6

THE SECRET OF OVERFLOWING HAPPINESS

"If you are not happy here and now, you never will be."

—TAISEN DESHIMARU

Happiness is in high demand.

There is a shortage of happiness in the world. The majority of poor people wish for money, believing that it will bring everlasting happiness. Many rich people are bored after satisfying their every desire and whim. They are further from happiness than even the very poor.

If we sit back and reflect upon our circumstances, we will sooner or later come to the conclusion that possessions alone will not bring happiness. Nor will the lack of possessions necessarily bring misery. If this were the case, then the poor would always be miserable and the rich always happy. But the reverse is often true.

Some of the most miserable people I know are rich. Some of the smartest and happiest people I've met have only the barest of necessities. Many people who have accumulated great riches say that the selfish gratification that followed ended up robbing life of its sweetness—and that they were never as happy as when they were poor.

So, what is happiness and how can we possess it? Is it real?

THE MISTAKE OF DESIRE

Many people believe that the only way to happiness is by the gratification of desire. This belief is rooted in the soil of ignorance, watered by selfish cravings, and is the cause of all the misery in the world.

This word *desire* does not just mean the baser, more sensual cravings in life, but extends to the higher psychic realm, where the cravings are even more powerful. These desires deprive people of the beauty, harmony, and purity of soul that is happiness.

Most people will agree that selfishness is the cause of all unhappiness in the world, but they believe it to be *someone else's* selfishness and not their own. When you are willing to admit that all your unhappiness is the result of your own selfishness, you will be close to the gates of paradise.

As long as you are convinced that it is the selfishness of others that robs you of joy, then you will remain a prisoner in your self-created hell.

Happiness is that inner state of perfect satisfaction—joy and peace—from which all desire is eliminated.

The satisfaction gained from gratified desire is brief and always followed by an increased demand for more gratification.

Desire is as insatiable as the ocean. It yells louder and louder for your attention. Desire demands ever-increasing service from those who are blinded by its temporary rewards.

Finally, its followers are exhausted and break down with physical or mental anguish. Desire is the region of hell, and all torments are centered there.

Giving up desire is the realization of heaven, and all pleasure awaits there.

"Happiness is that inner state of perfect satisfaction from which all desire is eliminated."

A POEM

I sent my soul through the invisible
Some letter of that afterlife to spell
And by and by my soul returned to me,
And whispered, "I myself am heaven and hell."

HEAVEN AND HELL WITHIN

Heaven and hell are states of mind. Sink into self and gratification of desires and you will sink into hell. If you rise above self and into that state of consciousness that forgets self, you will enter heaven.

When you pursue your own desires, you are without true knowledge. This always leads to suffering. Correct perception, unbiased judgment, and true knowledge are obtained only when you are in the divine state. When you realize this divine consciousness, then you will know true happiness.

If you selfishly seek your own personal happiness, it will continue to elude you and you will be sowing the seeds of misery. When you lose yourself in helping others, happiness will come to you and you will reap a harvest of pleasures.

ANOTHER POEM

It is in loving, not in being loved,
The heart is blessed;
It is in giving, not in seeking gifts,

We find our quest.
Whatever be your longing or your need,
That do you give;
So shall thy soul be fed, and you indeed
Will truly live.

GIVE TO GAIN

If you cling to yourself, you are clinging to sorrow. Let go of yourself, and you will enter into peace. To seek selfishly is to lose happiness. Even if you obtain that which you thought would bring you happiness, it will not satisfy you.

The glutton is continually looking for a new delicacy to stimulate his deadened appetite. Finally, after becoming bloated, burdened, and diseased, food of any sort rarely tastes good anymore.

People who have mastered their appetite neither seek nor think of tasty pleasures, yet find delight in the most frugal of meals.

The illusory form of happiness is seen through the eyes of self and found through gratified desire.

When embraced, it is always revealed to be the skeleton of misery.

Truly, "he that seeks his life shall lose it, and he that loses his life shall find it."

Lasting happiness will come when you are ready to sacrifice. When you are willing to lose that impermanent thing that is so dear to you—and it will be snatched from you regardless someday—then you will find happiness. That which seems like a great loss now will become a great gain.

To give up in order to gain—to be willing to yield up and suffer loss—this, indeed, is the way of life.

"To give up in order to gain—
this, indeed, is the way of life."

HUNTING HAPPINESS

How can we find happiness in things that, by their nature, will pass away? Real and lasting happiness can be found only by centering ourselves in that which is permanent.

If you rise above the desire for temporary things, you will become conscious of the eternal. Then, by growing more and more in self-sacrifice and universal love, you will become centered in that consciousness. You will discover happiness that has no reaction and that cannot be taken away from you.

The heart that has reached utter self-forgetfulness in its love for others has become possessed of the highest happiness. It has entered into immortality for it has realized the Divine.

Look back on your life, and you will discover your happiest moments were those when you were doing things for others.

Spiritually, happiness and harmony are synonymous. Harmony is a phase of the Great Law whose spiritual expression is love. All selfishness is discord. To be selfish is to be out of harmony with the Divine.

As we realize that all-embracing love that denies self, we find ourselves increasingly in harmony with the divine music, the universal song, that indescribable melody. We find true happiness.

Men and women are rushing here and there, searching blindly—madly—for happiness. They can't find it, nor will they ever find it, until they realize that it is within them and all around them. It fills the universe, but they, in their selfish seeking, are closing the door on it.

THE SECRET OF HAPPINESS

I followed happiness, to make her mine,
Past towering oak and swinging ivy vine.
She fled, I chased, o'er slanting hill and dale,
O'er fields and meadows, in the purpling vale;
Pursuing rapidly o'er dashing stream,
I scaled the dizzy cliffs where eagles scream.
I traversed swiftly every land and sea,
But always happiness eluded me.
Exhausted, fainting, I pursued no more,

But sank to rest upon a barren shore.
One came and asked for food, and one for alms;
I placed the bread and gold in bony palms.
One came for sympathy, and one for rest;
I shared with every needy one my best;
When, lo! sweet happiness with form divine,
Stood by me whispering softly, "I am thine."

—BURLEIGH

Sacrifice the personal and temporary and rise into the impersonal and permanent. Give up your own desires and enter into the company of angels and the heart of universal love.

Forget yourself entirely in helping others, and divine happiness will free you from all sorrow and suffering.

"Taking the first step with a good thought, the second with a good word, and the third with a good deed, I entered Paradise."

You also may enter Paradise by following the same course. It is not somewhere up in the sky; it is right here. It is found only by the unselfish.

If you haven't experienced this unending happiness, you might begin by holding the idea of unselfish love. Think it over. Consider what it means to you—what it might mean to people you know. Then start trying to actualize this idea in your life. Aspire to it.

By aspiration, the destructive forces of desire are changed into divine energy. To aspire is to consciously avoid desire. It is the prodigal son, made wise by loneliness and suffering, returning to his father's mansion.

GOOD TIMES GIVING

As you rise above yourself and break the chains that bind you, you will begin to realize the joy that comes from giving. It becomes a glaring distinction from the misery of grasping. Give of your substance, your intelligence, and the love and light that are growing within you.

You will then understand that it is indeed "more blessed to give than to receive." The giving must be from the heart and without any desire for reward.

The gift of pure love has always been accompanied by pleasure. If your feelings are hurt because you are not thanked or flattered after giving, then you were prompted to give by vanity instead of love. Check your motivations. You were giving to get; you were not really giving but grasping.

Lose yourself in the happiness and well-being of others. Forget yourself in all that you do. This is the secret to everlasting happiness.

Always question your motivations and be on guard against selfishness. Learn the lessons of inward sacrifice.

You will climb the highest heights of happiness, remain in the sunshine of universal joy, and be clothed in the shining garment of immortality.

REFLECT

- Possessions alone will not bring happiness. It is possible to be poor and very happy or rich and quite miserable.

Happiness can be obtained by...

- Admitting that unhappiness is the result of your own selfishness.
- Recognizing that gratifying a desire will not bring happiness—only more desire.
- Eliminating all desire and cultivating inner peace and harmony.
- Focusing on helping others.

For this reason, you must...

- Forget yourself in service to others.
- Hold the idea of unselfish love in your mind, and then actualize it in your life.

DISCUSS

What is happiness to you?

If you made more money, had a bigger house, a nicer car, etc., would you be happy?

Are you relying on things outside yourself to bring you happiness?

Is happiness only in the future—an afterlife perhaps—or can there be happiness on earth?

Do you remember times when you gave of your time, money, or talent to help others? How did giving make you feel?

Is it possible to be happy right now, always?

CHAPTER 7

THE REALIZATION OF PROSPERITY

"It is wealth to be content."

—LAO TZU

Prosperity—like happiness—is not an outward possession. It is an inward realization.

It is realized only by a heart that is filled with trust, integrity, generosity, and love. A greedy man may become a millionaire, but he will always consider himself poor as long as there is a man in the world who is richer than himself.

A generous and loving man will be full of prosperity and riches even though his outward possessions may be few.

He is poor who is dissatisfied; he is rich who is contented with what he has, and he is richer who is generous with what he has.

When we think about how the universe is full of good things—materially and spiritually—then compare that with man's blind eagerness to pile up money or have for his own a few acres of dirt, we see the depths of our ignorance and selfishness. Selfish seeking is self-destruction.

Nature gives everything freely and loses nothing. Individuals grasping at all lose everything.

"Prosperity is not an outward possession. It is an inward realization."

REAL SUCCESS

Don't fall into the belief that you must do all that it takes—right or wrong—in order to become successful. Don't allow the word *competition* to shake your faith in goodness.

Wrongs will be made right under the unchangeable law.

Under all circumstances, do that which you believe to be right. Trust the divine power in the universe, and it will not desert you. You will be protected. Losses will be turned into gains and curses into blessings.

Never let go of your integrity, generosity, and love. This is what will lift you into the state of prosperity.

Don't believe those who tell you to "look out for number one" and put others second in your life. This is selfishly seeking your own comfort. It won't bring happiness; it will only bring eventual loneliness.

Instead, let your soul expand; let your heart reach out to others in generous warmth. Your joy will be enormous and lasting.

All prosperity will come to you.

People who have strayed from the path of goodness worry about competition. If you always pursue what is right, you don't need to worry about it. That's no empty statement. There are plenty of people out there who, by the power of faith and integrity, have conquered all competition.

These same people have risen steadily into prosperity, while those who tried to stop them have fallen back in defeat.

When you possess these qualities that make up goodness, you have put on the armor that defends against the powers of evil.

You will be protected through every trial, and you will build a life of success that can't be shaken.

You will enter into a life of prosperity that will last forever.

REFLECT

- Prosperity is not an outward possession. It is an inward realization.

True riches can be found by...

- Filling your heart with trust, integrity, generosity, and love.
- Focusing on all the good things, materially and spiritually, in the universe.
- Discontinuing the pursuit of success for selfish gain or competition.

Trust in the Divine, and you will be protected...

- Losses will be turned into gains and curses into blessings.
- You will be lifted into the state of prosperity.
- Your soul will expand, and your joy will be everlasting.

DISCUSS

How can you cultivate a daily practice of gratitude?

Have you been pursuing success for selfish reasons (power, possessions, prestige, etc.)?

How can you inject more purpose into your pursuit of prosperity?

What is the true definition of prosperity?

How will you apply the lessons contained in this book to build a life of success?

What additional actions can you take to support your journey to prosperity?

AFTERWORD

This has been a presentation of James Allen's *The Path to Prosperity.* We here at Sound Wisdom hope you've enjoyed the experience as much as we have.

Within these pages, you have just consumed powerful wisdom—magic even.

Do you want the cure to your problems in life? Like Dorothy's ruby slippers, which signified her power to grant her deepest desire, the key to happiness is already yours.

Observe the working of the laws of the universe, which always return our efforts to us according to our intentions and actions. Make use of childlike faith to believe in true goodness. Harness and direct the mental energy to shift your habits of thought.

Find prosperity within and around you.

The choice to live a meaningful life is yours and yours alone.

www.ingramcontent.com/pod-product-compliance
Lightning Source LLC
LaVergne TN
LVHW020646100826
845148LV00012B/2352

* 9 7 8 1 6 4 0 9 5 1 4 0 2 *